IB SOC
CULTURAL ANTHROPOLOGY

IB SOCIAL AND CULTURAL ANTHROPOLOGY:

A STUDY AND TEST PREPARATION GUIDE

PAMELA S. HALEY, PH.D.

BrownWalker Press

Boca Raton

IB Social and Cultural Anthropology: A Study and Test Preparation Guide

Copyright © 2016 Pamela S. Haley
All rights reserved.

No part of this book may be reproduced or transmitted in any form or by any means, electronic or mechanical, including photocopying, recording, or by any information storage and retrieval system, without written permission from the publisher.

BrownWalker Press
Boca Raton, Florida • USA
2016

ISBN-10: 1-62734-605-8
ISBN-13: 978-1-62734-605-4

www.brownwalker.com

Table of Contents

Chapter 1: Introduction 1

Chapter 2: Ethnographies 5
In Search of Respect: Selling Crack in El Barrio 5
The Riddle of Amish Culture 6
Shadowed Lives: Undocumented Immigrants in American Society 6

Chapter 3: Internal Assessment 13
Observation Report 13
What to avoid in your observation 15
Critique 19
Limitations of the observation 20
Criterion B: Description and analysis 24
Criterion C: Focus, assumptions, and bias 27
Criterion D: Critical reflection 28

Chapter 4: Paper 1 31
Strategies to score high on Paper 1 31

Chapter 5: Paper 2 35
Criterion A (Conceptual knowledge and analysis 37
Criterion B (Use of ethnographic material) 40
Criterion C (Comparisons) 43

Chapter 6: The Importance of Writing 45
Comparative Writing 48

Chapter 7: Final Thoughts: Social and Cultural Anthropology is More Than a Test! 51

Appendices
Appendix A: Sample Class Syllabus 55

Appendix B: Internal Assessment Requirements 58
Appendix C: Sample Internal Assessment
Observation Report...59
Appendix D: Internal Assessment Directions 62
Appendix E: Internal Assessment Ethical Guidelines........ 63
Appendix F: Critique Model... 65
Appendix G: Marks for Critique... 68
Appendix H: Critique Checklist 70
Appendix I: Paper 2 Model Response for first essay 71

Chapter 1

Introduction

I have taught standard level International Baccalaureate Social and Cultural Anthropology (IBSCA) Standard Level for about 12 years. During those 12 years, only two students failed the exam, and that was in my first years. But through the years, I have studied every (well, many) aspects of social and cultural anthropology (SCA), and I plan to keep studying it until I draw my last breath.

Unlike some disciplines, social and cultural anthropology is very easy to connect to our daily lives, because SCA is not just studying other cultures; it is about learning about all humanity, including ourselves. Specifically SCA explores how we think, judge, interpret, and analyze humanity. In a sense, we are all anthropologists. We all observe other people; we look for patterns; we compare one group to the other; some of us even record our observations in a journal or diary. And "certified" anthropologists do all of that, too. But the difference between the experienced and certified anthropologists and everyday anthropologists is that formally trained anthropologists make a conscious effort to rid themselves of biases, assumptions, and moral judgments when observing others. In addition, they often spend years studying a specific group. The study the history and past ethnographies. It is not uncommon, for example, for anthropologists to spend their entire academic careers studying one group or even subgroup of people. They learn the language, history, kinship patterns, and every aspect of the target culture. They live and work among their target populations and gather numerous informants who will teach them about the target culture. Yet, they would never proclaim that they are the expert on that people. They, instead, humbly admit that their study is merely a detailed cultural account at a specific time and place. No more, no less.

Anthropologists may be a humble group readily admitting to biases and rejecting absolutist conclusions. On the other hand, the study of social and cultural anthropology can change your life, because it can deeply change your worldview. It can make you a keener observer by giving you the tools to observe people and human interactions from a more objective and analytical stance. It does this by training you to observe not only explicit culture, but the more elusive, and much more interesting, *implicit* culture. Social and cultural anthropologists are always looking for implicit culture perhaps even more so than explicit culture. Therefore, hopefully you will find yourself looking for more implicit cultural indicators such as gender relationships, power hierarchies, societal structures, inequalities, kinship relations, et cetera. Explicit culture is more "in your face', so to speak. It is what the culture presents for us to see. For example, explicit culture would be marriage ceremonies and all the ritual and ceremony that go with them. Most American informants, for instance, could easily describe a traditional middle-class mainstream marriage ceremony where the bride wears a white dress and the groom a dark-colored tuxedo. But anthropologists look more for the implicit. They may ask why there is such a stark differentiation in the dress of the bride and groom especially on the wedding day. Even though women wear pants in everyday American attire, why on this particular day would a bride never wear pants, at least in the traditional heterosexual marriage practice? Why does the bride carry flowers and not the groom? What is the historical context behind the American wedding ritual? How did it evolve? Why is the male and female bodily presentation so starkly differentiated? What are the symbolic meanings of this performance? What about all the props, for example the flowers, the gifts, the church itself, the religious aspect, the performance roles? As you can see, I could go on and on. And that is what an anthropologist does. They look deeply into any human performance, whether it is a formal ritualistic performance like a wedding, or an informal one like a neighborhood gathering. All human interactions are interesting to curious anthropologists, especially the implicit, the questions or topics generally not discussed openly or not a part of the usual discourse. Implicit cultural displays are always ripe for anthropological investigations.

One more final point about the importance of social and cultural anthropology. As briefly mentioned above, this subject has the potential to change your life, because it has the potential to change your worldview. Like most Americans, before I began studying SCA, I had a rather rigid and limited worldview. I am not proclaiming that today I have an infallible grasp on the world and its inhabitants. Far from it. But I have learned that the world is a complex sphere with over seven billion inhabitants and too many cultures and subcultures to quantify. And these numerous groups are constantly in a state of flux. Grasping even the comprehensive knowledge of even one group of people is a monumental task. But SCA can make you more aware of the scope of human understanding and make you a keener and more critical observer of the human condition. And with this awareness, comes a much needed dose of humility, and with that humility you may become more tolerant and less judgmental of others, while becoming more cognizant of your own limitations.

I love social and cultural anthropology, so I admit that I am terribly biased in my assessment of this subject. I do not see how anybody could not absolutely love this subject, because when we study anthropology, we are studying ourselves. And we all have a little narcissism within us, so who could not fall in love with anthropology? However, I also have to admit that some of the ethnographies I have read have put me to sleep within five minutes. One of the reasons for the tedium is that ethnographies have to go into great detail about a group of people in order to present that group in a comprehensive manner. Still, if you hang in there and do not give up, you will learn a great deal not only about the groups you are studying, but about yourselves. It is also my intention that using my suggestions, whether you are a teacher or student, will help you avoid the monotony of some ethnographies. Therefore, I have chosen three of the most interesting ethnographies that exist today. And one of the reasons they are so appealing is that two of them are very controversial as well as having their fair share of sex and violence, something that Americans tend to be drawn towards. So, get ready for a fascinating ride into the captivating world of social and cultural anthropology. The next three sections will discuss the three main ethnographies that will prepare you for your IB examination. Keep in mind that you do not have to use these particular ethnographies. You can choose any three that you find interesting. I merely suggest the following ones because most of my former students and I have found them fascinating along with being effective in preparing for the IBSCA examinations.

CHAPTER 2

ETHNOGRAPHIES

In Search of Respect: Selling Crack in El Barrio
by **Philippe Bourgois**

In Search of Respect: Selling Crack in El Barrio is the first ethnography I teach for the course. Sometimes I teach the full ethnography; other times I only use Bourgois articles that I have found online or in different anthropology readers. I chose Bourgois for several reasons. First, he engages students by taking them to a place most of them have never been, and that is into the dangerous and illicit world of illegal drugs. In the culture we inhabit, students are curious about the drug underworld, so the material immediately grabs their attention. Also, Bourgois is the pre-eminent authority on the drug underground economy. In addition, there are plenty of supplementary web materials including Bourgois interviews, YouTube videos, Quizlet quizzes, and podcasts. Students and teachers alike tend to love this ethnography. I must add a word of caution here: If you are very conservative, or squeamish, or are teaching students who come from a very conservative background, you may be wise to get permission from your school's administrators before reading *In Search of Respect*. However, there are several IBSCA courses that use Bourgois with great results on the IB examinations.

To accompany Bourgois, students view Stacey Peralta's documentary film called *Crips and Bloods: Made in America*. This film thoroughly supports Bourgois' thesis, although Peralta delves more into African-American resistance to American societal norms. The film can be found on Netflix or other online outlets. Both Bourgois and Peralta pay close attention to the historical globalization factors that forefront loss of US manufacturing jobs and is a precursor to the unrest in poor neighborhoods. Each looks at structural underpinnings of inequality such as poverty, racial discrimination, and urban apartheid that coalesce to create an often volatile situation in America's cities. For Peralta, you can get a historical context synopsis on line by googling his work. After Bourgois and Peralta, I do a "180" and begin teaching about the Old Order Amish of Lancaster, Pennsylvania, explained in the next section.

The Riddle of Amish Culture by Donald Kraybill

The Amish may be said to be the complete opposite of gang society. Here the student is taken from a violent, cruel, and often dysfunctional world riddled with drug usage, conflict, abuse, and even murder into a seemingly ideal and almost utopian world where the Old Order Amish somehow seem to escape the many dysfunctions of modern American society. Students enjoy comparing these two societies and exploring how two American subcultures with very different values can both live within one American society. In my opinion, Donald Kraybill's *The Riddle of Amish Culture* is one of the most interesting, comprehensive, and effective ethnographies to prepare for the IBSCA exam. Kraybill meticulously studies the Old Order Amish of Lancaster, Pennsylvania.

I teach *Riddle* for many reasons. First, Kraybill is a superb writer, laying out his argument in an easily understood format. Second, the ethnography covers many themes listed in the International Baccalaureate Social and Cultural Anthropology guide such as agency, community, society, social reproduction, modernity versus tradition, social change, et cetera. Third, if we could label anyone an expert on a people, it would be Donald Kraybill, who is not an anthropologist, but a sociologist, which is fine because social anthropology is very closely related to sociology. In fact, I received my master's degree in sociology. So the two disciplines can be used interchangeably for your IBSCA examination. Fourth, there is a free online *Riddle* Instructor's Guide that fully explains how to augment exciting and interesting lessons, in addition to helping students comprehend the subject matter. Fifth, a wonderful and comprehensive PBS film called *The Amish* from *The American Experience* series, nicely accompanies *Riddle*.[1] This film has authentic Old Order Amish photographs and commentary from Amish scholars including Kraybill himself, so it is the perfect academic companion to *The Riddle of Amish Culture*. Sixth, *Riddle* is the best ethnography I have found for preparing students for the examination. In fact, I was first introduced to Kraybill by students whom referenced him on the IB exams. I noticed that students who had read Kraybill usually did quite well on Paper 2 of the exam. Therefore, I started using *Riddle,* and I have used it for several years with great success.

There are also a few themes that you need to pay careful attention when reading *The Riddle of Amish Culture*. First, anytime Kraybill compares the Amish to US culture, pay careful attention as this gives you a solid background for comparing two groups, an important scoring criterion that you will read about later. You may think that because you are from the US, and, of course, feel totally immersed in US culture, that there is not anything you could possibly learn about American culture. But remember, all of us are like fish in water, which does not see itself in water, until it gets outside of the water. The fact that we are deeply embedded within our own culture, keeps us from observing ourselves objectively. Our culture feels so "natural" to us that we no longer see it, like a fish in water. Kraybill's Amish study forces us to come outside of our individual worlds and see ourselves from another perspective. And this is one of the beauties of *Riddle*. Second, pay particular attention to how Kraybill explains culture change. One of the "riddles" in the book is how the Amish have changed culturally despite being extremely resistant to change. Cultures are never static, not even the Amish, and Kraybill successfully illustrates how the Amish have dramatically changed through the years. The chapters on tourism need to be read very carefully, be-

---

[1] *The Amish: The American Experience* can be found online.

cause they are excellent illustrations of how the Amish have effectively adapted to changing environments. You need to understand how cultural contact has changed the Amish both economically and socially.

I can only think of one challenge in reading *The Riddle of Amish Culture*. When I first distribute the book to my classes there are a few moans and groans, because the book is almost 400 pages, which is considered quite lengthy for an ethnography. But I tell them to fear not, because we will be skipping or skimming some chapters. In addition, Kraybill has added a huge appendix which covers around 70 pages, a testament to his exhaustive research, by the way. And, for those of you who become enamored with the Amish, by all means, read the entire book. The rest of you can skip Chapters 6-9 and still have a deep understanding of the Old Order Amish of Lancaster, Pennsylvania.

Shadowed Lives: Undocumented Immigrants in American Society by Leo Chavez

I cannot think of a more important ethnography than *Shadowed Lives: Undocumented Immigrants in American Society* because of the political climate that we see today in terms of the backlash against undocumented immigrants. Emotions are strong about US immigration policy, so as I introduce this ethnography, I remind my students that a basic underlying anthropological principle is to be open-minded and attempt to rid yourselves of assumptions, biases, judgments, and prejudices. I also ask them not to judge a book by its cover, because to look at *Shadowed Lives*, your first thought is apt to be that this book looks really boring. It is a rather small book (which students like), but the cover is very nondescript, the print is rather small, and the photographs are in black and white. However, the book is beautifully written after one gets through the historic details. In fact, Chapter 6, "Green Valley's Final Days" is a model for excellent anthropological writing, especially the conclusion which he entitles "Final Thoughts." I strongly suggest that you use this ethnography not only to educate yourselves on the plight of undocumented Mexican and Central American immigrants, but to understand how an author effectively presents a strong argument. Therefore, focus on how Chavez sets up his argument, which will be discussed more fully in the next section.

Shadowed Lives: Undocumented Immigrants in American Society concerns a controversial topic with strong emotions on both sides of the argument. Remember when reading this ethnography, we are not debating if undocumented immigrants (UIs) should have a right to be in the United States. Chavez is merely giving you a snapshot of undocumented immigrants' struggles when migrating to the US and how they were treated when many migrated to the United States in the 1980s. He begins his argument by educating us on the historical relationship with Mexico. Great historians have said that if one does not understand the history of a topic, one does not understand the topic. Again, we see the importance of the historical context in understanding Mexican migration, so make sure you are very clear on the historical context. Chavez spends a lot of time on historical context at the beginning of his ethnography, so I encourage you to summarize the historical relationship between Mexico and the US as you will be expected to include historical context in both Papers 1 and 2. Unlike Kraybill's *Riddle*, there is no Instructor's Guide to go along with this ethnography, but there are some wonderful films about Mexican border crossings. I use *Wetback: The Undocumented Documentary* by Arturo Perez Torres, a graphic depiction of the risks some Mexican and Central Americans take when they cross the border.

Another reason I encourage students to read *Shadowed Lives* is because, like *The Riddle of Amish Culture*, it offers insightful avenues for comparisons. Chavez indirectly compares the destitute UIs with the affluent San Diegans. On a macro-sociological scale, Chavez is comparing what happens when developing world citizens come into cultural contact with the developed world. In this case we are referring to some the poorest of the developing world coming into close contact with some of the wealthiest of the industrialized world. Keep in mind that Mexico itself is considered by social scientists to be industrialized; still Chavez is targeting the poorest of Mexican and Central American citizens.

Shadowed Lives also provides a voice to a population that has had little voice, and therefore no power, in American society. One of the approaches that anthropologists take when studying a society is to always ask: Who has the power? The UIs have so little power, and have been portrayed by some media outlets and politicians as being less than desirable, that I wanted students to understand another perspective.

Another important reason for reading *Shadowed Lives* is that undocumented immigrants inhabit virtually every state in the US; therefore they affect all of our lives in some form or fashion. For example, here in South Florida I have had the privilege of knowing several undocumented immigrants. I feel extremely close to this topic as do many of my students. In fact, a few of my students are undocumented themselves or have undocumented relatives, so the interest level is exceedingly high. Most of my students have been totally engaged in the topic, many presenting personal stories of struggles or interviewing undocumented family members or friends. You may be thinking that I have a positive bias associated with undocumented immigrants. And I admit that I do have a positive bias towards UIs; however, it is only after I studied them that I acquired this bias, and hopefully you will too!

I have now introduced you to the ethnographies I think you will like, and I believe will thoroughly prepare you for the IB-SCA examination. However, there are hundreds of ethnographies that cover a variety of cultures and topics, so I encourage you to explore and find one that you particularly like. Remember, whether you are a teacher or student, if you are interested in something, you will be a more enthusiastic learner. For teachers, if you have a passion for or interest in a particular group, by all means incorporate that into your curriculum. In fact, the first few years of teaching IBSCA, I encouraged students to choose one ethnography on their own, write about how it connects to IBSCA themes, and present it to the class. That is how I discovered *Shadowed Lives*. I also have included major cultural events into my lessons. If a major cultural event takes place, I will search for an ethnography or article that helps my students and me to understand the event. For example, when Michael Brown was killed in Ferguson, Missouri, I found the ethnographic works of sociologist Victor Rios appropriate to help explain these events. SCA is a very flexible academic discipline with multiple approaches and resources and is easily adapted to current events. There is something for everyone in this exciting subject whether you are a teacher, student, or just a curious person. The next chapter explains how to complete your internal assessment.

CHAPTER 3

INTERNAL ASSESSMENT

Observation Report

The IBSCA Internal Assessment equals 20% of your IBSCA grade. During the first few weeks of the course, your instructor will tell you to observe a place where humans interacting with their environment and each other. You will be asked to take notes and write a report of the observation that is between 600-700 words. Suggested venues could be a classroom, bus stop, airport, restaurant, train station, park, nursing home, sporting event, or just about anywhere where human social interactions are taking place. However, make sure that you have permission from your instructor before committing to a location. I remember one of my students decided to observe a ladies' restroom. She hid in a restroom stall and peeked out to observe the women. She wanted to see if women were more likely to wash their hands when others were present. Interesting idea, but she clearly violated anthropological ethics because she invaded their privacy. More importantly she failed to criticize her methods in her critique. Because of these shortcomings, she was severely penalized in her Internal Assessment score. Make sure to check with your teacher if you have any doubt about ethical violations.

The only criterion for the observation is to be detailed and organized. This may sound simple and straightforward, but it is more complicated than meets the eye. First, you must decide if your observation will be context or issue-based. Context-based means you are focusing on a place be it a classroom, bus stop, et cetera. Issue-based means that you are focusing on an issue such as ethnicity, gender, or rites of passage. The important point is that you focus sharply on whatever you choose. For example, if you choose context-based, make sure you focus on a small enough area that can be easily managed. If you choose a restaurant, for example, focus on a specific section of the restaurant such as the bar, dining, waiting, or kitchen area (if available), et cetera. Do not try to write about the entire restaurant, unless, of course, it is very small. Also, avoid observing a place where you work, because it is difficult to work and fully observe at the same time. If you did do this, however, you must address the difficulties entrenched in this methodology such as inherent distractions and bias.

Second, let us reflect on the word *detailed*. A detailed observation report should provide the reader a clear and concise image of the area that you have observed. In fact, there will be so many details that you should have a difficult time confining your write-up to 700 words. So, observe very closely. Thoroughly describe the setting, time-frame, and actors. Note interactions between actors and between actors and cultural artifacts. Note anything that stands out, referred to as outcroppings by anthropologists.

Third, we need to examine the word *organized*. In the context of writing your observation/report, *organized* means to put your notes into some kind of logical order. An ineffective order that some students have chosen in the past is to merely describe observations in chronological order. I would not recommend this method, as these students tend to score low for Criterion A. Instead I suggest that you think about some logical categories. For example, you may begin your observation by describing the setting in terms of where (specific place) and when (time and date) you observed your subjects. You could even include your methodology or how you went about observing such as focus (context or issued-based) and materials used (notepad, smart phone, et cetera), and your physical position (where you were sitting when you recorded the event). Depending on how much detail you use for each of these topics, you could describe them in either one or two paragraphs. Of course, if you do not include these topics, you should deal with their exclusion in your critique on your paragraph about methodology. The last sentence of your introductory paragraph should be your thesis statement. In one sentence the thesis statement tells the reader the focus of the observation. Refer to Appendix C to see an example of a thesis statement, which in this case is the next to the last sentence of the introductory paragraph.

The next paragraphs could be devoted to the interactions you observed. Here you could organize your observations into two paragraphs: (1) actors' interactions with artifacts; and (2) actors' interactions with other actors. Subsequent paragraphs could be devoted to any behaviors that stood out to you or patterns that you noticed. Finally, you could do a bit of analysis of what you saw. I state *could* because this is neither required nor necessary. However, if you have not reached the 700 word limit, you may want to consider doing a bit of analysis. Do not worry about a formal conclusion, because with an observation report, you do not need one. If you want to have a concluding statement, you could state what time the observation ended as your final statement.

What to avoid in your observation

There are a few common errors I have observed through years of teaching IBSCA. First, avoid multi-tasking while observing. You may be tempted to look at your phone or some other device or listen to music during your observation. I would strongly advise against this, because it may cause you to miss important details. Remember sight is not the only sense you should use when observing. What you hear and even smell are critical and could provide important details for your observation. Generally, electronic devices distract from being fully aware of your surroundings, so I suggest turning all electronic devices off as they could distract you from being fully aware of important details.

As mentioned, I would also avoid conducting your observation at your place of employment or at any place where you have had some kind of personal participation. Again, it is nearly impossible to focus on your subjects and perform another activity at the same time. Similarly, observing a classroom while being a student in that classroom is also difficult and apt to be filled with assumptions and bias. For example, observing a religious service in which you are a participant is rife with limitations and distractions. One of the problems is that not only are you distracted by having to participate, but your vantage point may be blocked or limited in some way, again curtailing the details of the observation. Therefore, the best observations are at locations where you can have the most objective and unvarnished view as possible. Keep in mind that if you do observe a familiar situation in which you are also a participant, you can always address these inherent biases and assumptions in the critique.

Next, do not procrastinate. Transcribe your notes into your very rough first draft as quickly as possible. I advise this because the scene will be fresh in your mind, and you are more likely to accurately record your notes and to remember important details. Remember, that when you perform your observation, you are taking notes, which means writing fast and making abbreviations. Sometimes, you will be forced to leave out some details. If too much time elapses between the actual observation and the writeup, you are more likely to forget details. Remember, this will be your first draft, so it does not have to be perfect. Just try to organize it into some logical fashion and write about what you saw. Deletions, rearrangements, and additions can be done at a later time.

Summary of Observation Report

Notice that the directions and rubric for this activity are brief. This is done intentionally, because the point of the observation is for you to see how your views of human behavior will change after having had a social and cultural anthropology class. Do not worry about producing an anthropologically inspired observation. You are only required to observe for one hour and write about your observation in a detailed and organized manner and limited to 600-700 words. Lastly, be sure to insert the word count at the end of the document.

Here is a to-do list for your observation:

- Carefully choose place to conduct observation and avoid places where you work or would otherwise be.
- Decide if you want to focus on an issue or a place.
- Make sure there is social interaction.
- Follow anthropological ethics.
- Limit your scope so that you can be as detailed as possible.
- Decide on your methodology. (How am I going to observe and record?)
- 700 word count limit

At this point you need to STOP reading this chapter until after you have completed your observation and have taken copious notes. This is critical. DO NOT be tempted to continue reading as continuing will negatively affect the intended outcomes of the internal assessment activity. Remember, you will only be scored on details and organization. Now, proceed to perform your one-hour observation report, take as many notes as you can, and produce your first draft write-up.

At this point you should have finished your one-hour observation report and written detailed notes. Your first task is to reread your notes to see if all your writings are legible. Also, reflect back and make sure you included the setting, time, methods, and anything that stood out. Remember the importance of revising your notes as soon as possible after your initial observation. Time is the enemy of recall. So, I strongly advise you to read and reflect on your notes immediately after your observation.

Next, you should organize your notes into some kind of coherent and logical fashion. For example, your introductory paragraph should have included a detailed description of the setting, clarification of whether you chose an issue or context-based approach, and a one-sentence thesis sentence (This observation will focus on …). Then, divide your notes into some logical order.

Now you are ready to compose the first draft of your observation report. You may have to discard some of your notes that do not fit into an organized paper. Below is one way in which you could organize your paragraphs:

> Paragraph 1: setting, methodology, thesis statement
> Paragraph 2: interactions with people description and analysis
> Paragraph 3: interactions with artifacts description and analysis
> Paragraph 4: patterns
> Paragraph 5: outcroppings (behaviors or artifacts that stood out to you)

Remember that this organizational style is merely a suggestion. You may have an entirely different (possibly even better) organization style. The important thing is to have some type of organization. Also, you need one idea per paragraph, so make sure you can identify one obvious theme per paragraph. Being able to easily identify a paragraph's theme or main idea indicates your paragraph is focused and succinct. Focus and logical order will make for an organized paper.

After you have organized your paper, make sure you have enough details to give the reader a full and clear picture of what you saw. If you are much lower than the word count, add some more description or do more analysis. If you follow the paragraph suggestions from above you should have plenty of details. In fact, you will probably have too many details and will have to delete something. It is important not to go over the word count. You will not be penalized; the scorer will just stop reading after the word limit.

The next task is to proofread your observation several times for mechanical errors (spelling, punctuation, grammar, spacing). However, the main focus of your proofreading should be organization and details. Are paragraphs in a logical order? Is there a clear topic per each paragraph? Is your writing coherent? After you have finish several readings and have made appropriate corrections, I strongly suggest that you have a person well versed in written composition to give your paper another proofreading. Remember that good writing is largely rewriting. Careful proofreading is a major key to good writing! Please refer to Appendix C for a model detailed and organized observation report.

The Appendix C model observation report is very easy to score. First, it is both detailed and organized. Notice how the author provides a detailed description of the setting in the first paragraph. She also provides a detailed assessment of what the actors are doing and what they are wearing. The report is also well-organized using this organizational scheme: Paragraph #1 introduces the report by giving the setting. Paragraph #2 begins by describing how people are dressed. Paragraphs #3 and 4 give a detailed description of how people are interacting. Therefore, this particular Observation Report would receive the highest possible score for Criterion A, which would be a 5 out of a possible 5. Every candidate should easily be able to score at least a 4 for this criterion. Remember, it merely has to be detailed and organized to score full points for IA, Criterion A.

After completing all these tasks, you are ready to complete your final draft and submit your observation to your instructor. Your instructor will keep your observation report until a few months later when she will return your observation and instruct you to critique your initial observation report.

Critique
(To be read towards the end of the course, long AFTER you have completed your initial one-hour observation.)

I hope you followed my advice and have now completed your one-hour observation report and have submitted it to your instructor. The following section offers suggestions on how to complete the rest of your Internal Assessment which is a critique of your initial observation report.

The purpose is of the Internal Assessment is to get you to understand how just about everything you think you see is shaped by your own biases, assumptions, and a human tendency to categorize. What we think we see has severe limitations and the main purpose of the Internal Assessment is to get you to realize your own limitations as an observer. You probably are thinking, "No, I saw what I saw, and I know what I saw." Most of us feel this way. But we need only to look at eyewitness accounts to realize the fallibility of this line of thinking.

As alluded to previously, one of the aims of social and cultural anthropology is to get you to question what you think you see by making you aware of your own biases and prejudices. This is especially difficult for Americans socialized in the tradition where contemplation or deliberation is often viewed as weakness. However, what we think see, especially when viewing human interactions, requires a deliberate examination of how our own prejudices and biases shape our perceptions. What we think we see is reliant on what we have been taught or experienced. As Ralph Waldo Emerson said, "We only see what we are prepared to see." I would like to add some variations to that theme: We see what we want to see; we see what we have been taught or socialized to see; and we only see a partial view of any phenomenon. In fact, there have been numerous studies that demonstrate the variety of ways in which humans interpret the same event. Anthropologists know this, and even with this knowledge, they often revert to the human tendency to be absolute in their pronouncements of human behavior. More fallibilities and limitations of personal observations will be further explored in the next section.

Limitations of the Observation

Addressing the limitations of the observation will be an important paragraph in your critique. A one-hour observation has several limitations, and the scorers want you to recognize some of them. Hopefully you will be able to identify several, but since you only have 800 words, do not be surprised if you will have to omit a few or even several. The following will identify some important and obvious observation report limitations.

The first and most obvious is the **limited time period** in which you have been asked to observe some social phenomenon. How can anyone do any kind of meaningful observation in a one-hour time-frame? Understand that the latent purpose of the observation is not to observe for one hour and write down what you see. So what is the purpose?

To comprehend the purpose of the IBSCA Internal Assessment we will return to one of the IBSCA aims, which is to recognize our own preconceptions and biases. To explain assumptions and preconceptions, or often misconceptions, we can turn to IBSCA's sister class, Theory of Knowledge. One of the main considerations in Theory of Knowledge is the overarching question of how we know what we know. In other words, one purpose of TOK is to get students to constantly question where knowledge originates, how it is formed, and how it is reproduced. Indeed, as suggested above, the human senses are not reliable agents of knowledge. Just about everything we see or experience is open to various interpretations. Again we can see this scenario play out with the recent (2015) Ferguson, Missouri social unrest.

What was seen with the killing of Michael Brown was dependent on one's belief system shaped by one's personal experiences. Because the US is still largely ensconced in a cultural racial segregation, or what Philippe Bourgois refers to as "urban apartheid," African-Americans largely viewed the Ferguson events as police brutality, while many Whites viewed the events as justifiable homicide. Even the police officer may have shot Michael Brown because of the way he had been socialized to view African-Americans. In fact, Officer Darren Wilson himself stated that Michael Brown looked like a "big demon" coming towards him, even though there was little difference in the sizes of the two men. Both were above average in height and weight. Wilson's description of Michael Brown is very telling. Would Wilson have reacted the same had Michael Brown been White? Why did Michael Brown look like a demon to Officer Wilson? Perhaps something in Officer Wilson's background or experience had socialized him to be afraid of people who physically resembled Michael Brown, and unfortunately Wilson's reaction resulted in a killing. All of us are bombarded with news reports of crime, and these reports could teach us to be afraid of "the other," and in this case, the others are young African-American males.

Now, let us examine Michael Brown's perceptions. Perhaps Michael Brown learned that police were to be feared at best or hated at worse. According to Officer Wilson, Brown and his companion paid no attention to Wilson's commands to stop, and then "mouthed off" to Wilson. My point here is that everything that we see is biased dependent upon our ideological belief system, what our culture has taught us, or our individual or group experience. In the Ferguson episode, each social actor seems to have interpreted the other as aggressive or threatening. Maybe the result would have been different had each player examined his biases and prejudices.

I am assuming that you did not witness a killing while doing your observation. However, you probably did make several assumptions. Even a one-hour time-frame is ample time to make several assumptions and judgments, and the scorers want you to recognize and discuss those assumptions and judgments. So, in your critique of your initial report, you must recognize any assumptions, judgments, or preconceived notions that you may have had or made during your observation. Let us begin with your choice of venue. Merely choosing where and what to observe could suggest some sort of bias. For example, many Americans tend to be drawn to young people (youth-centric American society); both males and females tend to be drawn to males (patriarchal society); and then there is the issue of your own personal preferences that draw your eyes towards something you find interesting. In my 10-plus years of teaching IBSCA the usual venues chosen for the observation are places that students like to go or places where they work. In fact, many students like to perform their observations at their schools or workplaces. (Choosing a familiar place, by the way, is usually obvious to the scorers because of overlooked details that familiarity breeds. Still, if you decide to go this route, I would devote a fully detailed paragraph in your critique explaining that flawed methodology.)

Now, let us prepare for how we will critique this observation. Make sure you have the Scoring Criterion and a copy of your observation report in front of you as we go through this. Let us begin by asking some basic questions as seen below.

- What venue did you choose to observe?
- Did you focus on certain issues such as race and ethnicity?
- Do you live in a culture that emphasizes racial and ethnic differences?
- Did you fail to even notice ethnic/racial differences?
- Did you notice racial/ethnic differences for some, but not for others?
- Did you focus on males instead of female, or females instead of males, or ignore gender altogether?
- Did you concentrate more on females' appearance than males'? For example, did you describe how the women wore their hair, but made no mention of men's hair?
- Did you focus on a specific age group?
- Were there social actors in your view that you completely ignored?
- Did you focus on the physical appearance like being thin or overweight?

Your focus could indicate a cultural or individual preference which could indicate a cultural or individual bias. As previously discussed in the beginning of this section, your choice of venue could be an indication of preference. Categorizing social actors into racial or ethnic groups also has cultural and individual implications. So identify your focus and the terms you chose to categorize people in one or even a few paragraphs. Then, ask yourself why you identified or categorized people into certain groups. What does that say about you? Moreover, in a one-hour observation, how could you possibly know the racial or ethnic identity of your subjects? Did you interview them? Or did you merely *assume* that identity? I hope you are beginning to see a pattern here. The point for the observation is NOT to learn about the group or culture that you are observing, but to learn about yourself as an observer who makes assumptions or ignores details because of cultural or individual values. What you observed suggests more about your own preferences, prejudices, judgments, and assumptions than it does about the subjects you are observing. In other words, the purpose of this observation exercise is for you to see how you are highly affected by your culture or individual ideology. So, there is much more to this one-hour observation than meets the eye, and this is what IB is trying to teach. And this recognition is what IB is looking for in your Observation Critique.

The last issue with the Appendix C Sample Observation Report is the word count which is 61 words over. Not bad, but the scorer will stop reading at about 700 words as they do not want to give an unfair advantage to more lengthy reports. Obviously you would not critique this, but you would want to strive to keep your word count within the limit. Now we are going to apply scoring criteria to the Appendix C Observation Report. We will begin with Criterion B because we have already scored Criterion A.

Criterion B: Description and analysis

This criterion asks the observer to recognize and discuss the differences between descriptive inferences and sound analysis in a detailed and fully developed discussion. Here IBSCA scorers want you to demonstrate that you know the difference between descriptive inference and sound analysis. You do this by pointing out where you objectively described, made sound analysis, or inferred. As alluded to above, practically none of our observations are fully objective and are riddled with assumptions, judgments, and prejudices dependent upon our individual or cultural upbringing. So let us assess each Appendix C Observation Report paragraph in terms of description and analysis. Bear in mind that you may see something that I do not, so avoid interpreting my comments as anthropological canon, but merely as suggestions of another observer. (*Remem-*

ber to have Appendix C Observation Report in front of you as we complete this exercise.)

The following are some comments I would raise in preparation for writing a critique of Appendix C Observation and Report.

Generally, in terms of description and analysis, the entire report is mostly inferred description, deeply influenced by the writer's assumed American culture. The first paragraph is probably the most objective as the author describes the setting with no attempts at analysis. The author, however, loses her objectivity starting in the second paragraph and continues her subjectivity throughout the report. Throughout most of the observation report, she attempts to analyze, but her analysis is full of assumptions, judgments, and even has a moral condemnation-like tone.

First, let us look at the author's focus. She begins her description focusing on men's apparel and pointing out the large "bellies" that protrude over pant waists. Then she describes the women commenting on the women's large bellies, and even assuming that the women are wearing the loose-fitting tops in order to hide their protruding bellies. Two things stand out here: (1) The focus on weight suggests that the observer may have been socialized to view excess weight as a negative, a US cultural norm. (Historically some cultures have viewed excess weight favorably as a sign of health, wealth, and sexual attractiveness.) (2) She assumes that the women are ashamed of their large bellies and are, therefore, trying to hide them. This is an assumption because the observer has no way of knowing the subject's motivation for wearing loose-fitting tops. She conducted no interviews nor heard any conversation that suggested otherwise. So, her attempts at analysis are deeply flawed, and would fall under the category of descriptive inference as opposed to sound analysis.

Another issue with the second paragraph is the unbalanced description of the people waiting in line as opposed to the people serving the people waiting in line. Here again the observer's focus suggests that she places more importance on the consumers rather than the servers as she only provides one brief description of the workers in the last sentence. A more balanced analysis would have included more descriptions of the workers. For example, she could have addressed the following:

- Differences in clothing apparel between the workers (uniforms) and consumers, including the matching caps of the workers.
- Gender, racial/ethnic, age makeup of the workers versus the consumers? (Remember that commenting on this would require some assumptions on the observer's part. This is fine as long as these assumptions are identified as such.)

The observation also seems to disregard many worker details. We should emphasize not only what the observer saw, but also what she ignored. Maybe on a subconscious level she viewed the customers as more important than the workers. Or maybe in her past experience she had never actually worked at a movie concession, but she had stood in several movie lines. Individual past experiences influence the way one views events, and an astute anthropologist will recognize this.

The third paragraph is perhaps the most telling of the observer's biased perspective and can be identified as descriptive inference rather than sound analysis. Here she makes a moral judgment not only her subjects' weight, but also on their eating habits and food choices. She chastises them for buying junk food that she assumes contributed to their belly size. To make this judgment based on a one-hour observation is deeply flawed. How could the observer possibly know the diets of her subjects? Again, no interviews were conducted. She seems to draw her conclusions based merely on one of her subject's off-the-cuff comments about eating a lot of junk food. The observer does not know, yet she does not hesitate to judge. This is something that certainly needs to be addressed in the critique.

The fourth paragraph is purely descriptive and is similar to the first paragraph with seemingly no assumptions or judgments that I can see. Here the observer merely states what she sees and hears. For this paragraph I particularly like how the observer describes the conversation in the phonetic way in which she hears the words. This is always helpful when recording a conversation and provides the reader with a clear description of what the observer heard. Now we have discussed enough details demonstrating that we know the difference between descriptive inference and sound analysis.

Criterion C: Focus, assumptions, and bias

In addition to the blatant judgments made by the author of the Sample Observation Report, let us look more specifically in terms of critiquing this observation report. Let us begin with Criterion C, which asks the observer to be aware of the *position of the observer*. By *position of the observer* the scorers are not looking for where the observer sat or stood while she was conducting the observation, although physical positioning is important. Here they are referring to the *ideological position* of the observer. By now you should know that the ideological position constitutes the observer's beliefs, and these beliefs affect what the observer sees. So I would suggest that your critique devotes one fully developed paragraph on how your ideological position shaped what you saw. For example, for Appendix C Sample Observation Report there is evidence that the observer values body thinness and clothing apparel, because that was her main focus. She may also have a consumerist bias, because she largely ignored the people producing the food and drink. In addition, she seems to be somewhat ageist, because the tone of the report appears to ridicule older Americans. For example, someone from a non-ageist culture may have described the scene in an entirely different way, possibly commenting on how the elderly seemed to enjoy their night out at the movies; how they had healthy appetites; or how the men unselfishly stood in line trying to accommodate their appreciative wives. Similarly, someone with experience working behind a movie concession counter may have spent more time describing the workers as being polite and efficient despite harsh demands and ridicule from the customers standing in line. Therefore, as evidenced by her comments and focus, the observer's ideological perspective suggests that she values thinness, youth, and consumers, all US cultural values. Your job is to try to see how you observed from your own narrow ideological perspective and how this affected your observation. Hopefully you will come to agree with Ralph Waldo Emerson's 19th century observation that, "People only see what they are prepared to see." By now you should have a good grasp of Criteria B (description and analysis) and C (Focus, assumptions, and bias). Now, let us move on to the last criterion, Criterion D.

Criterion D: Critical reflection

Criterion D requires the observer (you) to reference anthropological concepts or methodological issues. Here the critique should reflect on the possibly flawed methodology used to perform the critique. In other words, how did you go about obtaining your data? For this criterion I would first describe the methods you used, and then I would examine the limitations of those methods. For example, the method you most likely used was to visit some site with a notebook, or smart phone, or tablet in hand and hopefully position yourself at a place where you could see and hear your subjects. One point here that you could address if appropriate, is permission from the owner of the establishment. I say appropriate because if you were at a large public event like a football game or concert, getting permission would not be necessary. However, the model observation took place in a movie theatre, and this venue would have required permission from the theatre manager. Or, if you were at a restaurant, you should have spoken with the manager prior to doing your observation. Therefore, the first thing to critique for this criterion would be permission issues which would require a sentence or two. The next part of this criterion addresses the limitations of your observation.

The most obvious limit of the observation report is the one-hour time-frame. One hour is not enough time to perform any type of meaningful observation or human behavior analysis. The next limit concerns how you went about gathering data. Most students take notes either on paper, an electronic tablet, or smart phones. All of these data collection tools require the observer to look down to record data. Therefore, you probably saw even less interaction every time you looked down to record notes. Looking down to record can cause the observer to miss important information. We already discussed how your ideological position influenced your observation, but another limitation could be your physical position. For the model observation presented in Appendix C, the physical position of the observer seems effective. She was close enough to hear conversations and to have a good view of her subjects. So, when addressing this Criterion, make sure you comment on your physical position in terms of its effectiveness in collecting your data. Note if your view or sound was obstructed or clear, and comment on it accordingly.

At this point you have more than enough ammunition to effectively criticize you Observation Report. You need to refer to the model Critique located in Appendix F. You may also want to take a look at the Internal Assessment Ethical Guidelines Requirements in Appendix E. A formatting checklist is located in Appendix H, and Appendix G provides an explanation for scoring.

Now you should feel confident in completing your critique. Remember to proofread a few times for content and writing conventions. Then, have a trusted friend perform another proofreading. The key to scoring a high mark on your Observation Report and Critique is to take your time to thoroughly observe; take detailed notes; reflect on what you saw; carefully read my suggestions and appendix models; type your critique; perform numerous proof readings; and submit your paper to your instructor. The next section of this book details the other IBSCA requirements, Paper 1 and 2 of the IBSCA External Examinations.

Chapter 4

Paper 1

Paper 1

Paper one counts 30% percent of your overall assessment and assesses your ability to interpret and analyze an ethnographic excerpt. You will be given a short ethnographic reading passage and will be expected to summarize and thoughtfully comment on the passage. After you read the excerpt, you will be asked three questions about the passage. The first and second questions are more or less reading comprehension questions where you address the question by summarizing or generalizing an aspect of the reading using your own words. Here the scorers are looking for you to not only paraphrase, but more importantly to demonstrate that you can "read between the lines." In other words, to perform a critical reading and make insightful comments. Question 3 will ask you to compare what you have read about a society to a different society that you have studied. You may want to address Question 3 first because Question 3 carries the most weight.

Strategies to score high on Paper 1:

1. **Be an active reader when reading the prepared ethnographic text.**
By "active reader" I mean a reader who reads with a pen or pencil in her hand. I would take about five minutes to skim the article and look at the questions, and 5-10 minutes to read the article closely. Circle key words; underline key phrases; and make notes in the margins. Look for hints of author's bias or assumptions. Remember that many anthropologists are from the West or educated in the West, and, therefore, have been

largely influenced by Western thought. In addition, all ethnographers have a somewhat limited view. So try to find some evidence of the author's limitations and spend a few sentences or paragraph detailing this. Again, I want to remind you not to be absolute in your pronouncements, but merely raise questions about the possibility of bias or assumptions. In other words avoid using vocabulary such as: *This proves such and such.* Or, *This shows that…*Instead use vocabulary such as: *This suggests…*; *The relationship could be because of…*; *The pattern could be a result of…*; *The author may be…*; *Perhaps the author is…* You get the idea.

2. Prioritize your response.

As soon as you look at the questions from the ethnographic excerpt, you will notice that there are three questions which are given various values as indicated parenthetically. The first two are given six points, and the last eight. Therefore, I advise addressing the last question first because it has the most value. Let us break down each question:

1. **Question 1** (Description and generalization) will ask you something about the text. Here you are expected to summarize and generalize, and basically to describe some situation from the text. Make sure you paraphrase. Direct quoting is fine, but make sure you place exact words within quotation marks. The scorers want to see how you synthesized the material, so use your own words. I advise my students to devote about 10 minutes to this question and usually write about one page depending on one's handwriting size.
2. **Question 2** (Analysis and interpretation) requires that you employ a bit more analysis to your response. Here you are expected to relate anthropological concepts. As mentioned above, here is your opportunity to apply some concepts you learned in class such as author's limitations, ideological or personal bias, or Western influence on anthropology. Look for ways to pick apart

the ethnographic material. If you cannot find any flaws such as Western bias or even an ethical violation, then focus in on some anthropological theme that you may have studied in class. This may include gender, inequality, cultural norms, ethnicity, class structure, conflict, socialization, power constructions, et cetera. The important issue for this question is to recognize that the anthropologist has a definite viewpoint.

Note that I have not included any sample Paper 1 responses in the appendices because of copyright issues. However, there are some samples you can find online if you google "social and cultural anthropology paper 1 samples."

3. Question 3 (Comparison) requires you to compare another society or culture that you have studied to the one presented in the text. Question 3 is basically an abbreviated Paper 2 response which requires you to identify the ethnography you are using in terms of name, author, timeframe, and historical context. You are also expected to make explicit comparisons and contrasts between the excerpt and one society you have studied. So do your best to apply similarities and differences between the two societies. Here you need to focus on one society. Trying to compare more than one society to the society in the excerpt will be difficult due to time constraints. I would devote about 20 minutes to responding to this question, and a few minutes proofreading all three questions.

CHAPTER 5

PAPER 2

Paper 2 counts 50% of your score. Therefore, this section is the most important in terms of how your final score will be calculated. On this section of the test, you will be given 10 broad essay questions where you will have to choose **two** to discuss within a two-hour time frame. So, this breaks down to approximately one hour per question. Each question addresses one or two of the IBSCA themes listed in the IBSCA Syllabus. However, from my experience certain themes appear more frequently. They are: power and resistance, gender, religion, kinship, migration, economic and political organization, modernity versus tradition, globalization, inequality, identity, ideology (belief systems). Now, keep in mind that you only have to answer two out of 10 questions. Therefore you should have an in-depth knowledge of at least three ethnographies that cover some of these themes.

Ethnographic knowledge is the basis for Paper 2. Recall that the IBSCA Syllabus states that IBSCA Standard Level candidates are required to have an extended knowledge of three ethnographies. These ethnographies can be studied in book, article, or film format. The ethnographies that I chose for my classes are "Work-a-Day World—Crack Economy" by Philippe Bourgois which can be found on line or in *Conformity and Conflict: Readings in Cultural Anthropology* by James Spradley and David W. McCurdy. "Work-a-Day World—Crack Economy" is an excerpted article from *In Search of Respect: Selling Crack in El Barrio*. In fact, Bourgois' work is one of the most popular ethnographies used by IBSCA teachers because of its appeal to teens and emphasis on power and resistance, economic organization, conflict, social class, globalization, migration, ethnicity, and inequality. I would recommend reading full ethnographies instead of short articles because of the in-depth analyses of reading a book as opposed to an article. However, the articles I mentioned are excellent if you are running short of time.

Besides ethnographic articles and books, anthropological films can convey anthropological concepts and principles in an interesting way. The films should supplement either an article or book being studied. A wonderful film that supplements Bourgois' work is *Crips and Bloods: Made in America* by filmmaker Stacey Peralta. Like Bourgois, Peralta captures the historical context behind the formation of the illegal underground economy. Keep in mind that if you are teaching in a conservative area, both Peralta's and Bourgois' works are chalk full of violence. In fact, Bourgois' *In Search of Respect: Selling Crack in El Barrio* has a rape scene that could be considered inappropriate for high school students. So be aware of your audience.

Paper 2 is the "meat" of your IBSCA Standard Level examination as this part of the test counts 50% of your total IBSCA testing score. Therefore, this section is the most important in terms of how your final score will be calculated. On this section of the test, you will be given 10 broad essay questions where you will have to choose **two** to discuss within a two-hour time frame. This breaks down into approximately one hour per question. Each question is worth a possible 19 points for each essay, and there is a possible six points across both essays for a grand total of 44 points for both essays. In other words:

Question 1	=	19 points
Question 2	=	19 points
Across both essays	=	6 points
Total	=	44 points

Each test question addresses one or two of the IBSCA themes listed in the IBSCA Syllabus. However, from my experience, themes that frequently appear are: power and resistance, gender, religion, kinship, migration, economic and political organization, modernity versus tradition, globalization, inequality, identity, ideology (belief systems). Now, keep in mind that you only have to answer two out of 10 questions. Therefore you should have an in-depth knowledge of at least three or four of these concepts and how they relate to the ethnographies studied. Let's begin by breaking down each assessment criterion beginning with Criterion A, which is worth six points and asks the candidate to demonstrate knowledge of anthropological concepts.

Criterion A (Conceptual knowledge and analysis)

For this criterion, the assessors are asking you to address the question using your knowledge of anthropological principles and core anthropological terminology. What does this mean? You can find a detailed answer to this by perusing the IB curriculum guide. If you cannot find the guide online, look for the IB Social and Cultural Anthropology Standard Level syllabus. This syllabus lists several terms and concepts; however, because you only have to address two of 10 questions, you only need a detailed knowledge of the core principles and terms addressed in the ethnographies you are reading. For example, some of the core terms and principles addressed by Leo Chavez in *Shadowed Lives* are: racial and ethnic inequality, migration, kinship, class conflict, globalization, assimilation, power and authority, cultural contact, ethnocentrism, and stratified societies. As you are reading your ethnography, note the anthropological themes that run throughout the ethnography. A good anthropology teacher will emphasize these themes. In fact, in my classes I introduce the themes before we read the ethnography making sure that students have some knowledge of the themes that are addressed in the ethnography.

An example of a Paper 2 question is: *Discuss how inequality is produced and maintained in one society you have studied.* Immediately you know that the theme to address is inequality. To address this question you should broadly define inequality. Then you should specify the kind of inequality you would be addressing. In this case it would be racial/ethnic as well as class, because in the case of *Shadowed Lives*, you have Central American and Mexican Native American groups (descendants of Mayan and Aztec cultures) migrating to the US in search of economic survival/opportunities. As you are discussing how class and racial/ethnic inequalities are inherent in American society, you would define what you mean. Astute students may even differentiate between how anthropologists define racial as opposed to ethnic. Another theme running throughout Chavez's excellent ethnography is power and authority. When studying a culture, a good anthropologist always assesses which group has the power and authority in a given society, and how that power is resisted and contested. In Chavez's work the Southern Californian white upper classes have the power in this San Diegan society, and Mexican and Central American migrants contest that power by crossing the borders without legal papers. In other words, the wealthy and affluent may make the rules, but the voiceless and powerless finds ways to get around those rules. So these themes of inequality based on ethnicity and class, power and authority and their concomitant resistance would need to be defined and discussed in relation to the ethnography that you are citing.

Another anthropological principle is the perspective of the social world as being interdependent and interconnected. Therefore, you must explain how the two cultures or subcultures you are studying are related. For example, Donald Kraybill's study of the Old Order Amish of Lancaster, Pennsylvania looks at how the residents of Lancaster rely on Amish tourism as a vital aspect of their economy and how the Old Order Amish have come to rely on the tourism for their cultural survival. Therefore, one focus of your reading should be how these two groups are connected. How do they depend on one another? By discussing these two groups, it is easy to make comparisons, using comparison cues such as *both, similar to, in contrast to, like, unlike,* and so on.

A third principle to always keep in mind is cultural relativism. This principle stresses the way in which we tend to judge other cultures based on our own cultural knowledge. A good anthropologist strives to eliminate or reduce moral or ethical judgments in relation to his or her own culture. Judging a culture by condemning or degrading a practice would be a violation of an anthropological principle, and therefore, you would be marked down. However, if you were to point out how the author made moral judgments in describing the target culture, you would be given points. For example, Napoleon Chagnon violates this principle in his work on the Yanomamo of South America. Chagnon refers to the Yanomamo as aggressive and violent people clearly using his own cultural standards to judge another culture. As you can see, making these kinds of assessments is also ethnocentric because he viewed the Yanomamo based on his own culture. In short, always be aware that we all observe other cultures and even our own culture through our own biased lens. So avoid violating this principle in your own cultural analyses, but if you observe it in another ethnographic study, by all means discuss it.

Other common mistakes or principle violations that ethnographers make is becoming too involved with the culture they are studying and/or violating anthropological ethics. The first rule of anthropological ethics is: Do no harm to one's subjects. Marc Fleisher illustrates this violation in his ethnography on Missouri street kids entitled *Dead End Kids*. Here, Fleisher gives cigarettes to a ten year-old informant. Even though the child was a veteran cigarette smoker, one could raise the possibility of an ethics violation. Did Fleisher harm this child by providing cigarettes? Keep in mind this is a rhetorical question and not one to be answered, but merely raised. Remember that one of the beauties of social and cultural anthropology is that it raises more questions than it answers. So look for ways the ethnographer you are reading violated a principle, but avoid at all costs making declarations of moral righteousness cued by using words such as *should*. For example, stating something along the lines of "Fleisher *should* not have given the child a cigarette." is making a judgment on the ethnographer's actions instead of raising a question. So avoid making these kinds of moral judgments against the ethnographer or another culture. However, I strongly encourage you to raise questions and even criticize an ethnographer as long as you have evidence to support your claims.

The final point that needs to be discussed for Paper 2, Criterion A, concerns how you structure your argument. Keep in mind that my suggestions are a template for a basic organizational framework. Good organization keeps you focused on your argument and makes your argument coherent and comprehensive. So the first task is to read the question at least two times and underline the key terms. These will be the terms that you will define, discuss, and relate to the ethnography. In the first paragraph I would define and discuss the terminology and briefly introduce how these terms relate to the question. Please refer to Appendix A for an example of a good introductory paragraph. To summarize Criterion A, make sure you have defined your terms, followed basic anthropological principles, and point out where the author of one of your readings may have violated some of these principles.

Criterion B (Use of ethnographic material)

The following section will focus on Criterion B which asks the candidate to demonstrate his/her ethnographic knowledge. Criterion B is worth the highest mark value of 8 points out of a possible 18. Use of ethnographic material receives the highest number of points; therefore, Criterion B is your first priority. To receive the highest score, you must present detailed, organized and relevant material that is fully identified in terms of author, time-frame, place, and historical context.

Ethnographic knowledge is the basis for Paper 2, and here is your opportunity to demonstrate your detailed knowledge of the three ethnographies you have studied. Recall that the IB-SCA Syllabus states that SCA Standard Level candidates are required to have an extended knowledge of three ethnographies. These ethnographies can be studied in book, article, or film format. The ethnographies I chose for my classes are "Work-a-Day World—Crack Economy" by Philippe Bourgois which can be found on line or in *Conformity and Conflict: Readings in Cultural Anthropology* by James Spradley and David W. McCurdy. "Work-a-Day World—Crack Economy" is an excerpted article from *In Search of Respect: Selling Crack in El Barrio*. Bourgois' work is one of the most popular ethnographies used by IB teachers because of its appeal to teens and emphasis on power and resistance, economic organization, conflict, social class, globalization, migration, ethnicity, and inequality. I would recommend reading two full ethnographies because of the in-depth analyses of reading a book as opposed to an article.

Besides ethnographic articles and books, as mentioned earlier, anthropological films effectively convey anthropological concepts and principles. However, films alone do not provide enough details to fully cover an issue and, therefore should be used only as a supplement to written ethnographies. The films I use supplement either an article or book being studied. A wonderful film that supplements Bourgois' work is *Crips and Bloods: Made in America* by filmmaker Stacey Peralta. Like Bourgois, Peralta captures the historical context behind the formation of the illegal underground economy as both attribute the underground economy to global forces. Both ethnographers attribute the rise of the underground economy to historical factors such as the loss of US manufacturing jobs which increased high unemployment and underemployment especially in minority neighborhoods. So, in addressing a question about inequality, globalization, economy organization, power, et cetera, *In Search of Respect* and *Crips and Bloods* offer multiple avenues for comparison.

The time-frame or what anthropologists refer to as "ethnographic present" is the time period in which the anthropologist actually studied the culture. This can be dealt with in one sentence in the introduction such as: "Bourgois studied the drug culture of Spanish Harlem, New York, in 1985 through the early 1990s in his classic ethnography, *In Search of Respect.*" Note that in this one sentence I included author, place, and ethnographic present, so all you have left to establish for the identification of material is the historical context.

Historical context can be thought of in two ways: (1) historical events at the time when the ethnography was written; and (2) the cultural history of the target group. Often these two approaches will overlap. Let us begin with the historical events at the time of the study. One of the ethnographies that I teach, *In Search of Respect,* was studied during the 1980s. So what was going on in the US at the time of this study? Recall that Bourgois' study is about the rise of the underground economy including the proliferation of illegal drug usage and selling in Spanish Harlem, New York. So the historical context applicable for Bourgois's study is the 1980s was a time of huge demand for cocaine in the developed world. To fill this demand in an increasingly globalized world, massive amounts of cocaine were being imported into the United States for illegal distribution. The drug trade was extremely attractive to some Americans especially those working at deskilled minimum wage jobs. These kinds of jobs were becoming more and more plentiful, because higher paying manufacturing jobs were decreasing rapidly as corporation relocated their factories outside the United States in search of cheaper labor and fewer environmental regulations.

The second approach to including historical context in your response is to explain the history of the cultural group. This constitutes a brief summary of the group that can be obtained from summarizing the history presented in the ethnography. Note that the ethnographer usually presents a brief history of the group at the beginning of the study. So all you have to do is summarize the summary and you have your historical context. A few sentences or a short paragraph will suffice in explaining the historical context. Whatever approach you use to incorporate historical context, make sure that the reader understands the relationship between the historical context and the purpose of the study.

I hope you are beginning to see the importance of historical context as the foundation of your argument. Historical context explains the underlying circumstances in which events occur, and is critical in understanding and analyzing whatever social group you are studying. As mentioned above, as you read your ethnographies, you will see that anthropologists begin their ethnographies with a history of the target culture. You will need to either introduce your argument by stating the historical context at the time the ethnographer studied his or her group, or be able to summarize the group's history as referenced by the ethnographer in the first section of the study.

Historical context is crucial in introducing your argument not only for both of your Paper 2 essays, but also for Question 3 in your Paper 1 essay, which I discuss in the Paper 1 section. So far I have stressed the importance of ethnographic knowledge, and suggested that you introduce your response by discussing the historical context. The next section will focus on Criterion C, which is your ability to make detailed and thoughtful comparisons.

Criterion C (Comparisons)

Comparing two groups *explicitly* is essential to scoring high on Paper 2. I emphasize explicitly because scorers do not want to have to look for your comparisons. Therefore, you need to use cues such as *like, unlike, similar to, in contrast to, both, neither*, et cetera which signals your use of comparisons. Criterion C requires candidates to provide detailed and hopefully thoughtful comparisons. Keep in mind that these comparisons do not have to be between two cultures or two works. They can be between two groups within the same society such as different ethnic or racial groups, men and women, young and old, and so on. Remember, that you need to demonstrate knowledge of at least three societies. In order to show knowledge of three societies, one essay could compare two works or ethnographies, and the second essay could compare two groups within one society. The best way for you to learn how to make comparisons is to follow my model located in the appendices.

By now you should have a good idea of how to prepare for this portion of the exam. And since this portion is worth 50% of the IBSCA examination final score, it is the most important. In other words, if you can score high on Paper 2, the chance of you passing or even scoring a five, six, or seven dramatically increases.

Chapter 6

The Importance of Writing

I cannot stress enough the importance of writing for every part of the IBSCA exam. In fact, I have had students from the past had mediocre knowledge, but had excellent writing skills, and they scored a five. Writing is important because it demonstrates logical and coherent thought. If your writing skills are low or mediocre, you need to sharpen those skills. Writing is a skill that is not only important for the IBSCA exam, but for every IB exam, every high school class, every college class, and on and on. So, how does one become a good writer?

It has been my experience that good writers are not born. It seems to come easier for some, but anyone can become a good writer with enough practice. You can become a good writer by following these suggestions:

1. **Know the basics.**

Spelling, grammar, and punctuation are important because they symbolize communication. Spelling, of course indicates a word. Do not worry if you place an *e* before an *i*, or something similarly insignificant. However, if your spelling makes the word illegible, then the thought can become incoherent. Grammar is important because incorrect grammar can change meaning. Sentence fragments and run-on sentences make your paper harder for the reader to comprehend. Both suggest jumbled and unfocused thoughts, leaving the reader confused. Run-on sentences are not sharply focused, leaving the reader confused. Punctuation also symbolizes meaning. Periods mean the end of a complete thought, while commas mean a pause. So, if you did not master the basics in elementary school, then go back and learn the difference between a period and a comma. Do not use colons or semi-colons if you are not sure how. A lack of basic writing skills suggests to the reader, maybe on a subconscious level, that you are a low level thinker.

2. Organize thoughtfully.

Focused arguments are well organized and sharply focused. Think about when you are debating a point in Debate Club, class, or even informally with a friend. The person who has the best argument states her thesis and then provides supporting evidence for their point. They do not go off on tangents bringing up irrelevant points. Therefore, stay focused on the question. A good way to do this is to highlight the key words from the question and then use those words to form your quick outline. Here is a sample question and quick outline to guide your response:

> Sample Question: *Discuss how inequality is produced and maintained in one society you have studied.*

First, define *inequality* and *society* (as opposed to *culture*). Then, ask yourself:

a. What are the inequalities within the Old Order Amish? (possible discussions points: gender, age, and church position)
b. What produces inequality in the Old Order Amish? (possible discussion points: ideological beliefs such as patriarchal religion and specified age hierarchy)
c. What maintains inequality in the Old Order Amish? (possible discussion points: religious and familial rituals and traditions)
d. How do the Amish compare to mainstream Americans in terms of inequality? (Similarities include mainstream patriarchal religious beliefs, although much more diverse in the mainstream. Differences include feminism and equal rights awareness, separation of church and state ideal, influence of pop culture).

e. How has inequality among the Amish changed in the last few decades? (Remember, you always want to discuss social change/transformation because that is a main anthropological theme and fully addressing it is worth four points on the Paper 2 exam.)

Referencing Kraybill, I would begin with something like this:

> *Kraybill's Old Order Amish is generally an egalitarian society (groups of people who share the same space) in the sense that community members generally have equal access to community resources. In other words, there is not a large economic gap between Amish farmers, factory workers, and tourist industry workers. However, economic disparities has changed over the last few decades as some Old Order Amish have become millionaires mainly due to selling goods to tourists. Some bishops have even chastised some "wealthy" Amish for having too many material goods and subsequently have asked them to "tone it down a bit."*

I would then proceed to address each point listed above.

Or, referring to Bourgois' work on crack cocaine in Spanish Harlem, you could begin with something like:

> *Inequality can be defined as the unequal distribution of resources in a given area where groups are interdependent and interconnected (society). In other words, inequality for our purposes can be defined as the resource disparities between the rich and poor. Inequality can be produced and maintained by racial/ethnic discrimination, urban apartheid (spatial separation determined by racial/ethnic characteristics), or inaccessibility to resources valued in a culture. In a capitalist society there is an inherent inequality because capitalism in its purest form creates a small wealthy class (those with more capital) and a proletariat class (those who provide the cheap labor to obtain that wealth). The highly educated (those skilled in a high demand service occupation) can rise to the wealthy class by learning skills necessary to perform a service that is in high demand, such as physician, doctor, engineer, or comput-*

er scientist. However, access to the training required for these occupations requires a vast amount of education beginning at a very early age. Children in poor neighborhoods are often denied access to the necessary training because they may be surrounded by drugs, crime, and poor schools. They typically end up remaining in those neighborhoods and the cycle of inequality is maintained through generations.[2]

There are also samples of Paper 2 responses that your teacher should be able to provide. If not, you could search for them online.

A basic hallmark of well-organized writing is to write in complete sentences that connect to one another. Each sentence and paragraph should flow to the next, and each paragraph needs to address your thesis. Have a guiding sentence per each paragraph, and make sure that every sentence in that paragraph is connected to the guiding sentence. There is a very high correlation between insightful thought and good writing skills.

Comparative writing

As alluded to in the first section of this book, for both Papers 1 (Question 3) and 2, you will be expected to compare and contrast. Therefore you should be familiar with the construction of a proper compare/contrast essay. A model for this type essay is in Appendices for Paper 2. Remember that your essay must *explicitly* compare. Again I stress explicitly because the scorers do not want to have to look for the comparisons; they should be clear. The obvious way to make comparisons or contrasts clear is to cue the reader with word such as: *like, unlike, compared to, in contrast of, both, neither, similar to, different from,* et cetera. As explained previously, remember that the comparisons and contrasts DO NOT have to be between two societies or cultures. You can compare women and men, age groups, cultures and subcultures, time periods, or approaches. If you are unsure

---

[2] Refer to Paper 2 Appendix for a fully developed response to this question.

about how to write a well-structured comparative essay, visit one of the many web sites devoted to this topic. Below I have listed some pointers on how to become a better writer.

1. Good writers read a lot.

You cannot become a good writer unless you are a prolific reader. Actually reading the ethnographies as opposed to skimming them is good practice. Sadly, many Americans are more concerned with speed than with deep and critical thinking. So slow down and read carefully. It is more important to read a few chapters carefully than the entire book quickly. More specifically you should pay close attention to how anthropologists construct their arguments. Both Donald Kraybill and Leo Chavez are excellent writers. As you read their works or other ethnographies, deconstruct what they do in each paragraph. Recognizing how others make solid arguments and then mimicking their techniques will make you a better writer. By the way, these writing skills you are learning and practicing now will help you in all your present and future academic endeavors.

2. Good writing requires a strategy.

Granted that this is a timed test, and you will only have one hour for Paper 1 and two hours for Paper 2. Therefore, you need a writing strategy. First, take a few minutes to sketch out an outline of the main points you want to make. The administrators provide as much paper as you need, so make sure you get an extra sheet for planning/mapping your argument. Then put those main points in a logical order. This will keep you focused. One of the common criticisms of IB exams, especially for Paper 2, is lack of focus. An unfocused paper equals a weak argument, and a weak argument equals a low score. Second, once you have outlined your arguments, begin making your argument in as much detail as possible. Try to refer back to the key words that you underlined in the question. Again, this helps you stay focused and reinforces your argument. Lastly and if you have enough time, take a couple of minutes to do a quick proofread of your essays. Often, a missing word or punctuation mark can change or confuse the meaning of your argument. Also, if you discover that you missed an important point, it is never too late to add that point in the margins.

3. What NOT to do.

In closing, here are a few more writing suggestions for all IB-SCA writing assignments. First, never begin your essay with grand pronouncements such as, "In today's world…" or "Since the beginning of time…" These are lame ways to begin a paper that scream to the reader, "Oh no! Here comes another trite elementary paper." Right away the reader has a negative bias. Second, use *active* verbs as opposed to *being* verbs. Too many variations of the verb "to be" (is, are, was, were, et cetera) make for an elementary sounding paper. Actions verbs are always more descriptive and specific. Third, use your best handwriting. If your argument is illegible, it will not be scored. If your handwriting is illegible, ask the teachers if you can type your response. I have scored a few papers that were typed because the student could not legibly hand-write the response. Fourth, do not obsess over spelling. Spell the word phonetically to your best ability. Also, keep in mind that writing per se is not an explicit criterion for any of the papers. On the other hand, focus and organization are all listed in the assessment, so practice well-organized and well-focused responses. If you practice good writing skills throughout the year, by the time you take the exams, you will be able to organize and express yourself in a more efficient and succinct way. You will feel more confident, and your argument will be more effective.

Chapter 7

Final Thoughts:
Social and Cultural Anthropology is More Than a Test!

This is perhaps the most important chapter of this book. I write this because, as mentioned previously, social and cultural anthropology has the possibility of changing or shaping your world view. It has the potential to change or shape your mode of thinking, and that changes everything. On a personal note, I was introduced to sociology and social and cultural anthropology in graduate school at which time I was in my 40s. This subject opened a new world to me and totally changed my outlook on life. All of a sudden, I felt as if I had an epiphany about how the world works. Much of what I had observed and experienced in my four decades of living started to make sense. Needless to say, I could not get enough of this subject. I ended up taking five graduate classes in sociology and anthropology just for my own personal enjoyment and love of the subject. So to reduce this life-changing discipline to merely passing a test is a great disservice. Therefore, I will end this book with the most important reasons to study anthropology: (1) you will become more sociologically aware; (2) you will become psychologically stronger; (3) you will enhance your career skills.

Sociological Awareness

By exposing you to other cultures, social and cultural anthropology will make you more aware of human rights. Although there are a few exceptions, anthropologists as a group are extremely aware of the importance of preserving and advocating for human rights. Many have seen the suffering of the exploited first hand by living for long periods of time with groups who have faced extreme oppression and poverty. Anthropologists are not likely to negatively judge those living in poverty or admonish the poor to "pull yourself up by your bootstraps." Once you become somewhat knowledgeable in anthropology, once you begin to look at the social structures under which the poor and disenfranchised live, you may begin to withhold your critical assumptions and judgments of others. Whether it is oppressed minorities or those migrating to other lands, you may find yourself less likely to harshly judge people who are trying to survive in an often cruel and unfair world.

As your understanding of and appreciation for other cultures deepen, you may find yourself growing personally. By studying groups like the Amish or undocumented immigrants, you will begin to more critically view your personal choices, for example how your consumption practices affect an entire chain chain of people who produced those goods. Who is picking that lettuce so readily available in Western grocery stores? Under what conditions were those jeans you just bought manufactured? Those old clothes you took to Goodwill, or that computer you threw in the trash, have an effect on others that few realize. Learning of the struggles undocumented migrants face on a daily basis may make you appreciate more what you have. Leo Chavez's *Shadowed Lives* details some of the most inspirational stories about the will of the human spirit to survive under some of the most horrific circumstances that few in the West have experienced. After my students read about the dangers of border crossings and heard a guest speaker describe her horrific journey from Mexico to the United States, they came to see undocumented immigrants not as criminals often portrayed by some cable news networks, but as inspirational testaments to human determination, ingenuity, bravery, strength and incredible familial love. For most of them, having to take an IB test, or perform any other unpleasant chore, suddenly took on a different meaning.

Learning about other cultures may also make you less sensitive to personal slights and insults. This is perhaps the most important latent function of taking a course in social and cultural anthropology. As you learn that human beings are products of social structures where they often have little or no control, and as you learn that we frequently misinterpret the action of others, you may be a little less likely to take offense when somebody personally offends you. At the very least, you may become more inclined to consider the broader context in which the offense occurred. Think of how many conflicts could be avoided if, instead of reacting aggressively towards a perceived slight or insult, you just let it go.

Even more importantly, understanding other cultures is of the utmost importance especially in today's turbulent world. Consider if the United States government had known more about the complexities of the Middle East, especially the huge cultural divide between the Sunni and Shia, perhaps we would have not been so quick to invade an area of which we knew so little. Maybe we could have saved billions of dollars and countless lives. Similarly, our idealistic view that the United States should spread democracy (a Western invention) throughout the world is ludicrous. Trying to impose one's own standards or values to a distance culture is the epitome of arrogance. Surly the current situation in Afghanistan, Iraq, and Syria have taught us a hard learned lesson in the dangers of interfering with other cultures.

On a practical note, IBSCA can enhance your skills in other disciplines. For example, since the IBSCA exam is totally essay bound, test preparation should consist mostly of writing assignments. Practicing written expression remains one of the most important academic skills. Indeed, SCA is a critical component of a well-rounded education whether you are entering medicine, law, or international business. One need only read Anne Fadiman's classic ethnography, *The Spirit Catches You and You Fall Down: A Hmong Child, Her American Doctors, and the Collision of Two Cultures*, to realize the ramifications of cross-cultural misunderstandings. And any international business person or lawyer can attest to the importance cultural knowledge when dealing with international clientele.

Social and cultural anthropology is so much more than a test. It can be a life-changing experience that will make you into a more cosmopolitan thinker and a humble world citizen with a broader global perspective. SCA hopefully will make you more compassionate, aware, and reflective, and less judgmental, ethnocentric, and egocentric. I hope you have enjoyed reading about social and cultural anthropology. I would love to hear from you, so feel free to contact me through Facebook and good luck on the test!

Appendix A

Social and Cultural Anthropology Class Syllabus

"People only see what they are prepared to see."
—Ralph Waldo Emerson

The Nature of Social and Cultural Anthropology

Anthropology generally is the study of humans. Social and cultural anthropology is the study of humans in a social and cultural context. Ethnography (a detailed written description of a culture or subculture) makes social and cultural a distinctive field of study with specific methods. These methods include a specific set of principles and procedures that an ethnographer will go about studying his or her subjects. Social and cultural anthropology is also the comparative study of culture and human societies. In other words, societies or cultures are studied by comparing them to other cultures or societies from both global and local perspectives. Increasingly social and global anthropology is concerned with urban and rural societies, human inequalities, and even aspects of modern nation states. Anthropology also contributes to an understanding of such contemporary issues as human violence, environment degradation, poverty, and human rights and injustice.

Goals

- Through ethnographic case studies, articles, and films, explore, compare and contrast specific societies and cultures.
- Recognize and apply ethnographic principles and procedures.
- Identify and reduce personal and cultural biases, assumptions, and prejudices.

- Understand how anthropologists describe and analyze cultures and societies.
- Apply understanding of anthropology terms and concepts to local and global relationships.
- Understand and explain processes of social and cultural change.
- Evaluate anthropological approaches, interpretations, and conclusions.
- Using anthropological principles, concepts, and terms, construct various forms of coherent written expression

Ethnographies

- Kraybill, Donald. (1989) *The Riddle of Amish Culture*.
- Chavez, Leo R., (1997) *Shadowed Lives: Undocumented Immigrants in American Society*.
- Other readings can be found online such as articles by Philippe Bourgois and Victor Rios.

Ethnographic Films

- *Crips and Bloods: Made in America*, 2000, Stacy Peralta
- *Wetback: The Undocumented Documentary*, 2004, Arturo Perez Torres
- *The Amish*, PBS American Experience, 2012, David Belton

Internal and External Assessments

- Internal Assessment (20%)
    - The internal assessment consists of a one-hour observation report of 600-700 words, and critique (criticism and analysis) of the initial report of 700-800 words.
    - Setting may be school, church, a restaurant, senior citizen facility, a club, train station, shopping mall, playground, et cetera.

- External Assessment (80%)
  - Paper 1 (30%)
    A one-hour written exam with three or four short-answer questions based on an unseen ethnographic text.
  - Paper 2 (50%)
    Two questions completed in a two-hour essay answered from a field of 10 questions of which the candidate will answer two.

APPENDIX B

INTERNAL ASSESSMENT REQUIREMENTS

- Perform a one-hour observation during the first few weeks of school without being given assessment criteria B–D. Students should only be given criterion A before writing the written report, which only requires that the initial observation be detailed and organized. The observation can be **context-based** or **issue-based**. Context-based is anyplace where there is public human interaction and has a specified function such as building lobby, transportation terminal, nursing home, store, park, restaurant, et cetera. Make sure students limit their focus in cases of large gathering places.
- The observation can also focus **issue-based**, such as gender roles, race, ethnicity, or rites of passage. However, issue-based observations must be grounded in concrete settings. In planning an **issues-based** approach as in, for example, gender roles or differences, race, ethnicity, or rites of passage, the topic needs to be defined in terms of specific groups and/or activities to ensure narrow focus and context. Both context-based and issue-based observations must be sharply focused.
- The observation may be conducted in small groups, but each student must undertake writing their individual observation reports. The written report and the critique must also be the student's own work. For both the observation report and critique, the teacher will stop reading after the designated word count.
- Type a 700-words observation report which should be given to the teacher who will retain it until a month or so before the course ends.
- The student will then complete another paper, of no more than 800 words, which critiques the initial observation and report. This includes an analysis and evaluation of the initial written report on the observation, produced approximately six months after the report.

Appendix C

Sample Internal Assessment Observation Report

Recall that the only criterion for the Observation Report is for your paper to be detailed and organized. So after jotting down notes while making your observation, make sure you have some sort of organizational scheme. The following is an example of a model Observation Report.

Observation Report

On September 10, 2015, at 7:30 p.m., I observed a group of about 30 to 40 people in the lobby of a movie theatre. The lobby of the multiplex was busy during this Saturday night observation with individuals milling around the lobby area. The lobby area contained a concession stand where some patrons waited in four long lines to buy popcorn, candy, and drinks. The other part of the lobby was decorated with six different movie coming attractions advertisements on the walls, colorful carpeted floors, and velvet ropes separating each movie venue. This observation will focus on the actions of the patrons and employees that I observed at the Regal 8 movie theatre located in suburban West Boca Raton, Florida. To appear as inconspicuous as possible, I sat near the concession stand near the front of the line.

The dress of the people waiting in line would be considered South Florida casual with the men wearing long or short khaki cotton or polyester pants with a mixture of polo, short-sleeved, Hawaiian-type button-up shirts. Most shirts were not tucked in as bellies tended to protrude over pant waists. Most shoes consisted of running shoes, some with Velcro strips fasterers or Docksider-type loafers. The women's attire was less uniformed than the men with a variety of clothing consisting of long pants, often black, with colorful tops of various styles, but, like the men, loose-fitting tops trying to hide rather large bellies. Another thing I noticed was that the women wore much more jewelry than the men to the extent that you could hear the jewelry jangling as they milled around the lobby. Women's shoes also consisted of more varieties than the men and included running shoes, flip flops, and leather sandals, for example. The workers had on uniforms of black pants, red polo shirts, and red baseball caps with the name of the movie theatre written on the front.

Most people in the lobby were standing in line waiting to buy various assortments of American junk food, which is snack foods with high fat, sugar, and salt content. The lines consisted of about eight people deep with most appearing elderly, for example between 60 to 80 years old. They were practically all Caucasian with whitish gray hair, and gender was female dominated with a ratio of about three to one. Many were overweight and probably shouldn't have been adding the pounds by eating junk food, especially popcorn which you could buy with extra butter poured on top. In fact, this seemed to be the most popular food as I heard several others request extra butter. One man yelled loudly to his overweight wife who was waiting nearby, "Myriam, ya want extra butta?" To which Myriam responded, "Yeah, Irv. Why not? Ya only live once. I'll start on my diet tomorra." A few people around Myriam nodded and chuckled in agreement.

One woman at the front of the line couldn't make up her mind what drink to order. She asked, "Do ya have any suga free soda?" The concession worker responded: "Yes Ma'am. We have Diet Coke, Sprite Zero, Diet Cherry 7-Up, and Diet Sunkist." "Could I sample Diet Sunkist?" the woman asked. "Yes, Ma'am." the worker responded. The woman took a sip, but still couldn't decide. The man standing directly behind the woman became visibly agitated and commented rather loudly, "Make up ya mind, lady! We haven't got all day!" The woman finally decided on the Sunkist soda. The worker then proceeded to scoop ice from a large ice machine and put it in a cup. The woman customer, intently monitoring the worker, said, "Miss, not so much ice. Save room for some soda." The worker dutifully poured a few ice cubes out of the cup and then filled it with soda. "That'll be $3.85." she said to the woman, who was now frantically searching for the right amount of change. She placed three one dollar bills and change on the counter, but could not seem to find the rest of the coins. At this point the man behind her took a quarter out of his pocket and impatiently placed it on the counter and said, "Here, for Pete's sake!" Some other people also appeared to be angry because of the long time they had been waiting in line. Another man kept looking at his watch and uttered, "How long can it take to put popcorn in a bucket? Jeez, we're gonna miss half the movie if they don't hurry up." The lines gradually decreased in size as the people scurried through the ropes to get to their chosen movie.

Word Count: 759

Appendix D

Internal Assessment Directions

- double space
- 12 font
- page number on lower right hand corner (Use footer.)
- last name and IB ID# on upper right hand corner (Use header.)
- Titles: Observation (Written Report) and Critique as headings on each paper
- Word count at end of each document (Observation 600-700; Critique 700-800)
- Compose title page (see link)
- 1 packet should consist of the following:
    a. cover page on top
    b. Observation Report in middle
    c. Critique on bottom.
- The Cover Page should have the following information:

Observation and Critique
International Baccalaureate
Social and Cultural Anthropology
Standard Level
Submitted by _____
IB ID #_____
Date of submission
Additional tips:

1. Address all parts of rubric (methods, description and analysis, assumptions and bias). Remember that these can overlap, but make sure you devote at least one paragraph to each.

2. Give examples.

3. Don't start any new analyses in the critique.

4. Note problems with methodological limitations (one hour, note-taking, ethical issues, etc.)

Appendix E

Internal Assessment Ethical Guidelines

Social and cultural anthropology students should consider these ethical guidelines before beginning their fieldwork and throughout the whole project. The following guidelines should be applied to all fieldwork. These apply to students preparing for internal assessment from 2010 onwards.

- Do no harm to the people who participate in fieldwork.
- Respect the well-being of humans and the environment.
- Obtain informed consent from the people who are the subjects of the fieldwork in a form appropriate to the context before you begin, providing sufficient information about the aims and procedures of the research.
- Fieldwork involving children needs the written consent of parent(s) or guardian(s). Students must ensure that parents are fully informed about the implications for children who take part in such research. Where fieldwork is conducted with children in a school, the written consent of the school administration must also be obtained.
- Maintain the anonymity of the people participating in fieldwork, unless participants have given explicit permission to the contrary.
- Store all data collected securely in order to maintain confidentiality.
- Be honest about the limits of your training.
- Do not falsify or make up fieldwork data. Report on research findings accurately and completely.
- Report your research findings to the people involved in your fieldwork.
- Do not use data for any purpose other than the fieldwork for which it was collected.
- Develop and maintain a working relationship with the people that you study so that other researchers can continue to work with them.

- Check with your teacher when the right way to behave is not clear.

APPENDIX F
CRITIQUE MODEL
Model Critique of Observation Report

Although detailed and well organized, my Observation Report has a few positives but also many flaws. These flaws include flawed methodology, ethical violations, unfounded assumptions, moralistic judgments, and biased focus. After providing a general critique, I will comment on each of these.

Methodological problems emerge at the start of my observation. First, my method of note-taking is somewhat flawed because of the difficulty in observing and writing simultaneously. While looking down to write notes, I could have easily missed some important interactions. Perhaps a video recording would have been more accurate, but recording would have required permission to film from the participants and that would have been all but impossible. In terms of ethics, although I did have permission from the theatre manager, I did not ask permission from the patrons or the employees, nor did I informed them. So, failing to inform subjects is an ethical violation, although for this type of observation, permission would have been next to impossible to obtain, because people were constantly moving in and out of the line. Perhaps it would have been better to confine my observation to the employees. However, there were a few pluses in my methods. My physical position was effective as I could clearly observe and hear the participants' conservations. Also I was not intrusive, because neither the employees nor the consumers seemed to notice me, as I easily blended in with my surroundings. Another positive aspect of my report concerns my effective use of direct quotations, because I quote exactly what I hear, instead of quoting standard English. My methods have both positives and negatives. However, the remainder of my report is riddled with biased interpretations of body presentation beginning in the second paragraph.

In paragraph two I describe the men's, women's and employees' dress. Although my descriptions of their clothing are generally accurate, my focus on the consumer's body weight is problematic as my comments reflect my Western cultural value of thinness, and therefore seem rather ethnocentric. It is clear here that I have internalized the commonly held American belief that an overweight person is not attractive, demonstrated first by my focus on weight in paragraph two and then continued in paragraph three where I make a condescending remark that the participants waiting in line "…shouldn't have been adding to the pounds by buying junk food…" This comment demonstrates some poor attempt at analysis and instead reflects my own ideological belief that thinness is more attractive on the human body. Moreover, I was making a kind of moralistic judgment that people *should* be more careful in their food selections and *should* avoid "junk food," a term, by the way, that I neglect to define.

Another issue with the entire report is my unbalanced descriptions. I tend to provide much more detail about the consumers than the employees. Looking back, the workers should have been described in much more detail, as the uniforms are symbolic of much anthropological commentary. Yet I only devote one sentence to the employees' dress and only report their conversation in relation to the consumers. I neglect to notice the relationship interactions amongstthe employees themselves nor their use of body language. This neglect suggests my consumer bias, possibly because I have never worked at a concession stand, but have often times waited in lines at movie concession stands.

I also rigidly distinguish the men from the women waiting in line, but because I didn't interview any of the participants, there is no way I could have been sure of their sexual identity, as it is increasingly difficult in modern society to make these distinctions. The same could be said of age, as I describe the participants as being between 60 to 80 years old, but I had no way of knowing this other than gross generalizations. Lastly, I commented that the subjects were "practically all Caucasian." This designation is problematic because as with gender and age, I had no way of knowing their racial identity. And even to attempt to categorize people based on race suggests more about me than about them. This tendency to categorize based on gender, race, and age suggests that I, again, may have internalized the American tendency to classify based on differences in human presentations of self.

Fortunately, most of my report was more descriptive than analytical, and therefore lessened the opportunities for problematic analyses which encourage faulty judgments. So my straight descriptions of clothing and conversation is effective in that my descriptions are well detailed and even include participants' individual word pronunciations as well as the subjects' body language adding to a more comprehensive image of events.

Word Count: 778

Appendix G

Marks for Critique

We will begin with Criterion B because Criterion A (Completion of the written report) was already scored. I suggest that on the Criteria rubric you highlight each in a different color. Then as you go through the critique, in the corresponding color, you highlight where the author references that criteria.

The highest score for Criterion B (Description and analysis) states that the critique both "recognizes and discusses the distinction between descriptive inference and sound analysis, and has provided examples in support of a fully developed discussion." For example, the author recognizes the distinction between the description and analysis in paragraphs three through six. However, the discussion is only partially developed. Therefore, Criterion B would score a three. Had there been one more detailed example, a four would have been awarded.

Criterion C (Focus, assumptions and bias) is scored a five because the author makes several detailed references to focus flaws, assumptions, and both her ideological and cultural biases. For example, the author recognizes that she has cultural bias of focusing on people's weight and even implicitly judging individuals' weight as a negative. She is correct in recognizing this as a cultural bias because many cultures look upon extra weight as attractive. In fact, you need only visit an old 1940-50s Sears and Roebuck catalog, and you would see that the models tend to be much heavier than models of today. So the author recognizes that she has taken on this cultural bias during her observation and recognizes it in her critique. Another bias she recognizes is her unbalanced focus on the consumers, or people waiting in line, and the concession stand workers. Here she correctly notes that she spends much more time on the consumers. She also correctly recognizes assumptions made in terms of gender, age, race and comments on each accordingly.

Lastly, Criterion D (Critical reflection) rates a five because the author spends the entire first paragraph fully detailing methodological problems while conducting this observation and relating these issues to her observation. For example, she briefly examines limitations such as note-taking and time, and critiques an ethical violation. She also addresses positives such as her physical position, lack of intrusiveness, and the way she recorded conversations. In addition, the entire critique demonstrates an anthropological understanding of the observation as she clearly recognizes her ideological biases.

APPENDIX H
CRITIQUE CHECKLIST

____Title: Critique

____Page numbers bottom right footer

____Word count at end of document

____Header: Name (last name first) and IB ID number

____Description and Analysis is addressed with appropriate examples

____Assumptions, bias, judgments addressed with appropriate examples

____Methodology addressed (flaws in methods)

____Organized (topic sentence with supporting details; paragraphs transitioned properly)

____12 basic font double-spaced

Appendix I

Paper 2 Model Response for First Essay

Question: *Discuss how inequality is produced and maintained in one society you have studied.*

Inequality can be defined as the unequal distribution of resources in a given area where groups are interdependent and interconnected (society). In other words, inequality for our purposes can be defined as the resource disparities between the rich and poor. Inequality can be produced and maintained by racial/ethnic discrimination, urban apartheid (spatial separation determined by racial/ethnic characteristics), or inaccessibility to resources valued in a culture. In a capitalist society there is an inherent inequality because capitalism in its purest form creates a small wealthy class (those with more capital) and a proletariat class (those who provide the cheap labor to obtain that wealth). The highly educated (those skilled in a high demand service occupation) can rise to the wealthy by learning skills necessary to perform a service that is in high demand, such as physician, doctor, engineer, or computer scientist. However, access to the training required for these occupations requires a vast amount of education beginning at a very early age. Children in poor neighborhoods are typically denied access to the necessary training because they are surrounded by drugs, crime, and poor schools. They typically end up remaining in those neighborhoods and the cycle of inequality is maintained through generations. Urban apartheid, a form of boundary maintenance, is one of the main themes in Philippe Bourgois' article "Workaday World—Crack Economy," (1995) and Stacey Peralta's film *Crips and Blood: Made in America* (2009). Both works deal racial/ethnic discrimination and class segregation.

The two ethnographic works are similar in that they both reference the loss of American manufacturing jobs as a contributing factor in civil unrest. In the 1950s post World War II era, the United States was virtually the only manufacturing country that had not been bombed during WWII. Thus, the US was the sole industrial power that exported its products on a global scale. US factories were booming and required skilled manufacturing wages. Unions kept the wages high and a large middle class was formed throughout the country. Blacks and Latinos filled many of these manufacturing jobs. Then came the 1970s social and economic transformations and the beginnings of more relaxed trade agreements and many corporations began to move their factories to the developing world. In addition, European countries had rebuilt their manufacturing base and Japan as well which made for more global competition. Gradually lower paying service jobs took the place of manufacturing jobs, unions lost their power, and the shrinking of the American middle class began. Many Blacks and Latinos were now relegated to the lowest paying and deskilled jobs that were proliferating across the American landscape.

Bourgois, who studied Latino/s African Americans in inner-city New York, explores how the underground economy, specifically the crack economy, impacted these inner-city youths during the 1980s and 90s. He argues that substance abuse is a symptom of an unequal society where poor kids of color are marginalized by the US society. From living in "the hood" for several years and forming close bonds with informants like Primo and Caesar, Bourgois discovers the struggles that families endured, such as single moms making meager wages, poor schools that didn't know how to deal with impoverished children, and the drug trade prominent on the streets of Harlem. He relates how Primo tried to find legitimate work in New York's financial sector, beginning as a mail clerk. During his first day of work his female boss called him illiterate, assuming that Primo didn't know what the word meant. He might not have known the meaning, but he knew he was being humiliated in front of the other employees. He also felt ashamed because he didn't have a dress shirt or tie to wear to work. Feeling disrespected, Primo eventually began selling drugs where he at least felt a modicum of respect from his fellow drug dealers in Harlem. Here Bourgois is trying to educate us on the deep rejection that these youths feel when they attempt to become integrated into the larger society. Because of what Pierre Bourdieu refers to as a lack of cultural (what one knows) and social (who ones knows) capital, the financial sector of New York felt like a different world to these kids, a world where they lacked the language, clothes, and skills to navigate successfully. In other words, they lacked the cultural knowledge and the social connections.

Similarly, Peralta found a lack of respect at the core of African-American youth disenfranchisement in South Central Los Angeles, California where his critique of America spans the 1950s through 1990s. Like Bourgois Peralta cites the loss of manufacturing jobs as an explanation for rise of drug dealing beginning in the 1970s. Unlike Bourgois, Peralta goes much deeper in his historical context as he goes back to the early 1950s where African-American youths tried to join the Boy Scouts and were rejected because of their race. They, therefore, formed their own groups which gradually evolved into heavily armed Crips who eventually monopolized the drug trade until the rival gang, the Bloods challenged their dominance. Again we see similarities to Bourgois as he attributes neighborhood dysfunction to poverty, drugs, segregation, discrimination, and lack of educational and career opportunity. In addition, like Bourgois, Peralta emphasizes the forces that keep these youths confined to their neighborhoods, a strong form of segregation and what social scientists refer to as boundary maintenance. Peralta also strongly emphasizes police harassment and even police brutality as young black men are pulled over and sometimes roughed up when they dared to venture out of "the hood."

So we see how racial and ethnic segregation with its inherent rejection by US mainstream society that keeps these youths locked into an environment where they see little opportunity of escaping. They're left with either a life of what Bourgois states as "slinging the mop for the white man", or other degrading jobs such as cleaning out pet crematoriums, or at best, slinging hamburgers at minimum wage fast food restaurants. Keep in mind that Bourgois emphasizes that the majority of inner-city youth do not engage in illegal activities. In fact, after living in the neighborhood, and seeing first hand what these youths endure, he doesn't understand why any of them would stay in the legal occupations. No wonder, Bourgois concludes, that these youths see the drug trade as more than merely a way to make quick cash, but more importantly to live a life with some dignity and respect.

Both Bourgois and Peralta offer valuable insights into the underlying causes that we see today in Ferguson, Missouri and several other venues across America, where it seems as though social inequality has not only been produced and maintained, but has gotten worse as the gap between the rich and poor seems to have widened since the 1980s and 90s. Both job outsourcing and manufacturing relocation continue to dismantle America's middle class, and minority neighborhoods continue to bear the brunt of these social changes. Media accounts of not only police brutality, but today even the militarization of the police force, lead us to consider the possibility that urban the apartheid is more harshly enforced in the beginning of the 21st century.

Marks for this response

Criterion A (Conceptual knowledge and analysis)

This response receives a 5 out of a possible 6. The paper clearly shows conceptual knowledge as several core terms are defined, discussed, and linked to ethnographic evidence. There is also some evaluation of Bourgois and Peralta as insightful ethnographers. However, there is no critique of core terms or ideas themselves. To receive a 6, the candidate would have had to have spent some time questioning or critiquing some of the core terms or ideas. For example, both Bourgois and Peralta seem to suggest that there is an Utopian type society could exist where all people are treated equally, and therefore live harmoniously without conflict or resistant. Is this possible in modern large scale cities? Look, for example, at China, a supposedly communist (equal) society, where inequality abounds throughout. To achieve a 6, the respondent would have to have a vast knowledge of world history and current events in order to convincingly question core anthropological principles. In fact, in my years of scoring IBSCA Paper 2s, I have rarely awarded a 6 for this criterion.

Criterion B (Use of ethnographic materials)

This response receives a 7 out of a possible 8. The response is clearly relevant and focused on the question with ample ethnographic evidence. The material is fully identified and complete in terms of historical context. Ethnographic presence is a little vague, however, as the author provides a general time-frame instead of specific one.

Criterion C (Comparisons)

This response receives a 5 out of a possible 5. Full points are awarded because detailed, relevant, explicit, and thoughtful comparisons and comments are easily seen throughout the entire essay.

Lightning Source UK Ltd.
Milton Keynes UK
UKHW020643111121
393791UK00011B/564